Our Newness of Life

The Spiritual Realm

By

CATHERINE PEARSON

LP CHRISTIANITY

ISBN 979-8888951422

TABLE OF CONTENTS

Introduction

In the book of **Galatians 3:1-3 (KJV),** Paul says, *O foolish Galatians, who hath bewitched you, that ye should not obey the truth, before whose eyes Jesus Christ hath been evidently set forth, crucified among you? Are ye so foolish? Having begun in the Spirit, are ye now made perfect by the Flesh? This only would I learn of you, Received ye the Spirit by the works of the law, or by the hearing of Faith?*

Our lives started from the Spiritual realm.

Paul asked the Galatians, "Are ye so foolish? Having begun in the Spirit, are you now made perfect by the Flesh? Most of the time, people read what Paul said to the Galatians and laugh, not knowing that we are doing the same things the Galatians did. "We began in the Spirit," Paul says yet many of us believers are unaware that our existence starts from the spiritual realm. We experience the physical universe through our flesh meaning, our physical bodies. Christians should live from the Spiritual realm.

This book centers on how Christians can live a life of victory starting from the Spiritual realm.

Where Do We Come From?

To understand where we come from, we must read the creation story. How God created the universe and mankind. According to **Genesis 1: 26-31 (KJV),**[25] *And God made the beast of the earth after his kind, and cattle after their kind, and everything that creepeth upon the earth after his kind: and God saw that it was good.* [26] *And God said, let us make man in our image, after our likeness: and let them have dominion over the fish of the sea, and over the fowl of the air, and over the cattle, and over all the earth, and over every creeping thing that creepeth upon the earth.* [27] *So God created man in his own image, in the image of God created he him; male and female created he them.*[28] *And God blessed them, and God said unto them, be fruitful, and multiply, and replenish the earth, and subdue it: and have dominion over the fish of the sea, and over the fowl of the air, and over every* *living thing that moveth upon the earth.[29] And God said, Behold, I have given you every herb bearing seed, which is upon the face of all the earth, and every tree, in the which is the fruit of a tree yielding seed; to you, it shall be for meat.[30] And to every beast of the earth, and to every fowl of the air, and to everything that creepeth upon the earth, wherein there is life, I have given every green herb for meat: and it was so.[31] And God saw everything that he had made, and behold, it was very good. And the evening and the morning were the sixth day.*

From the beginning, the first man, Adam, began a fellowship with His Father and was created in His Father's image and likeness because He was a Son of God. In the book of **Luke 3:38 (KJV),,** *which was the Son of Enos, which was the Son of Seth, which was the Son of Adam, which was the Son of God.*

God created everything after its kind from the beginning. The beast of the earth after its kind **Genesis 1:25.** *God made the beast of the earth after his kind, and cattle after their kind. Everything that creepeth upon the earth after his kind: and God saw that it was good.*

In **Genesis 1:21**, *The whale and every living creature that moves was brought forth after its kind.* **Genesis 1:24** *The earth brought forth living creatures after its kind.*

So, God formed His Son Adam after His image and likeness. So, God created Adam in His image and likeness.

God Is a Spirit

In the Book of **Luke 4:24 (KJV),** *God is a Spirit: and they that worship him must worship him in Spirit and in truth.* So, Adam was created after His Father's image with His nature and characteristics.

Adam was to function like His Father on earth, but he needed a body to live for him to function on earth. Therefore, God formed the body from clay/mud and put Adam in the body by breathing into his nostrils the breath of life; Adam became a living, Soul. In **Genesis 2:7 (KJV),** *And the Lord God formed man of the dust of the ground and breathed into his nostrils the breath of life; and man became a living soul.*

The word "breath" in this verse comes from a Hebrew meaning "Ruach," which means "Spirit." God breathed His Spirit into the body, and Adam became a living Spirit with a soul living in a body. In the book of James, the body must have a spirit. *For as the body without the Spirit is dead, so Faith without works is dead also.* **James 2:26 (KJV),**

Adam was a triune being he had a Spirit with a soul and living in a body. In the book of Thessalonians man is a triune being he is Spirit with a soul, living in a body. So, God put Adam, a Spirit, in the body (formed out of clay or dust) to give it life. In the Book of **1 Thessalonians 5:23 (KJV)**, *And the very God of peace sanctify you wholly; and I pray God your whole Spirit and soul and body be preserved blameless unto the coming of our Lord Jesus Christ.*

____

____

____

____

____

____

____

____

____

____

Man's Spiritual Fall

We saw Adam was a son of God, created in His Image and likeness. Even though he lived on earth, he was functioning from the Spiritual realm and in fellowship with the father. Adam disobeyed God and died spiritually, the beginning of all human physical deaths. In the book of **Genesis 2:15-17 (KJV),** *[15] And the Lord God took the man and put him into the garden of Eden to dress it and to keep it. [16] And the Lord God commanded the man, saying, Of every tree of the garden thou mayest freely eat: [17] But of the tree of the knowledge of good and evil, thou shalt not eat of it: for in the day that thou eatest thereof, thou shalt surely die.*

Genesis 5:5 (KJV), *And all the days that Adam lived were nine hundred and thirty years: and he died.*

Adam and Eve were separated from God after their disobedience. Adam and

Eve were no longer living from who they were; they lost their Spiritual life, identity as sons of God, and exalted position of righteousness.

Because they died spiritually, they started living from human nature/flesh, which became defiled after yielding to the enemy's lie. They became carnal, living in the Flesh.

The Flesh

The Greek word for Flesh is "Sarx," translated as Flesh in English with 4 meanings.

1. flesh or skin,
2. physical or natural body,
3. human or natural soul or natural mind unrenewed
4. Sinful natures in **Romans 8:6 (NLT):**

which the Bible calls,

a. Old Man - **Ephesians 4:22 (KJV),** *That ye put off concerning the former conversation the old man, which is corrupt according to the deceitful lusts. And be renewed in the Spirit of your mind. And that ye put on the new man, which is created in righteousness and true holiness after God.* **Colossians 3:9-10 (KJV),***Lie not one to another, seeing that ye have put off the old man, with his deeds; And have put on the new man, which is renewed in knowledge after the image of him that created him.*

b. Old self or former nature, according to **Ephesians 4:22 (KJV),***That ye put off concerning the former conversation the old man, which is corrupt according to the deceitful lusts. And* *be renewed in the Spirit of your mind. And that ye put on the new man, which after God is created in righteousness and true holiness.*

c. Sinful Flesh. In the Book of **Romans 8:3 (KJV),***For what the law could not do, in that it was weak through the Flesh, God sending his own Son in the likeness of sinful Flesh, and for sin, condemned sin in the Flesh.* Adam and Eve started living from Flesh which is canal.

The Greek meaning for carnal is "Sarkos," which describes anything Flesh, fleshy, natural, or unspiritual. Living from that state of carnality is death and enmity with God, and the Flesh cannot please God. According to **Romans 8:6-8 (KJV),** *For to be carnally minded is death; but to be spiritually minded is life and* *peace.*[7] *Because the carnal mind is enmity against God: for it is not subject to the law of God, neither indeed can be.*[8]

So then they that are in the Flesh cannot please God.

The word "please "comes from the Greek word "Aresko," which means "to be agreeable," so there is no agreement with God in the Flesh.

In the Book of **Galatians 5:17** *For the Flesh lusts against the Spirit, and the Spirit against the Flesh; these are contrary to one another, so that you do not do the things you wish.*

The Flesh and the Spirit are against or opposites to each other, so the Flesh can never agree with God.

In the Amplified Version, *For the desires of the Flesh are opposed to the [Holy] Spirit, and the [desires of the] Spirit are opposed to the Flesh (godless human nature);*

for these are antagonistic to each other [continually withstanding and in conflict with each other], so that you are not free but are prevented from doing what you desire to do.

The works of the Flesh are not of God, in the book of **Galatians 5:19-26 (KJV),** [16] *This I say then, walk in the Spirit, and ye shall not fulfill the lust of the Flesh.* [17] *For the Flesh lusteth against the Spirit, and the Spirit against the Flesh: and these are contrary the one to the other: so that ye cannot do the things that ye would.* [18] *But if ye be led of the Spirit, ye are not under the law.* [19] *Now the works of the Flesh are manifest, which are these; Adultery, fornication, uncleanness, lasciviousness,* [20] *Idolatry, witchcraft, hatred, variance, emulations, wrath, strife, seditions, heresies,* [21] *Envyings, murders, drunkenness, revellings, and such like: of the which I tell you before, as I have also told you in time past, that they which do such things shall not inherit the kingdom* *of God. ²² But the fruit of the Spirit is love, joy, peace, longsuffering, gentleness, goodness, Faith, ²³ Meekness, temperance: against such there is no law. ²⁴ And they that are Christ's have crucified the Flesh with the affections and lusts. ²⁵ If we live in the Spirit, let us also walk in the Spirit. ²⁶ Let us not be desirous of vain glory, provoking one another, envying one another.*

Living from the sinful nature has it's wages, which is death.

According to **Romans 6:23**, the original Greek word for "sin" is "hamartia, " a feminine noun. Which is sin nature. The nature we inherited has its wages which is death. For the wages of sin is death, but the gift of God is eternal life through Jesus Christ our Lord. The fall affected all mankind because we all came from the lineage of Adam.

In **Genesis 3:20,** *And Adam called his wife Eve because she was the mother of all living.*

We were all conceived from the lineage of a fallen man who had lost their identity as a son of God and their divine position of righteousness and was living from death. So, our lives began from death because we were separated from the life of God. Adam's disobedience brought death to all men.

In the Book of **Romans 5:12 KJV** *Wherefore, as by one man sin entered into the world, and death by sin; and so, death passed upon all men, for that all have sinned.*

The word "sin "in this scripture is not the action of sin that we commit, but rather a nature original Greek word for sin is "Hamartia," a feminine noun, which is the sin nature related to spiritual death. While "Hamartano" is a verb that is the action of sinful nature which produces the sinful actions or fruit of sin.

Therefore, just as through one person, sin entered the world and death through sin, and thus death spread to all men because all sinned. "Hamartano" is sinning. So, it's through Adam's act of sin that sinful nature entered the world and death through sin.

Through Adam's act of sin, the whole human race inherited the sinful nature that caused us to sin and die. So, everybody born from the lineage of Adam inherited Adam's sinful nature, which causes people to do the action sin. So, our actions of sins came because of the sinful nature we inherited from Adam.

The actions of sins didn't make us sinners but our sinful nature, which we inherited from Adam. According to **Romans 5:19 (KJV),** *For as by one man's disobedience many were made sinners, so also by one man's obedience many will be made righteous.*

It was Adam's disobedience that the whole human race was made sinners, not because of the actions of sins that made us sinners, but because of Adam's disobedience, we were sinners.

Adam's disobedience made us sinners, so we inherited his sinful nature, which caused us to sin.

Sinning is the fruit of the sinful nature we inherited from Adam. We all came from Adam, who was separated from God, and it's through him that we inherited his sinful nature, and that's why we sin.

Our actions of the sinful nature we inherited from Adam, who was separated from God, who is Holy and righteous in all His ways. In **Psalms 145:17 (KJV)** *The Lord is righteous in all his ways and holy in all his works.*

Man's spiritual fall resulted in inheriting a sinful nature, losing our identity as

Sons and our position of righteousness. All human beings were born from Adam's sinful nature, which is called the old nature, which is a translation of the Greek word "Sarx" and in the (KJV), is translated as "flesh."

Adam's disobedience made us sinners. So, because of Adam's disobedience, the human race started living from the Flesh instead of the Spirit realm, which was God's purpose and plan for all mankind.

So, God's arm provided a Savior, Jesus Christ, to accomplish His will here on earth. God's plan, even after the fall of man, was to predestinate man to be conformed to His image. Accordingly, **Romans 8:29 (KJV),***For whom he did foreknow, he also did predestinate to be conformed to the image of his Son, that he might be the firstborn among many brethren.* His Son is the express image of Himself, and every born-again human being conformed to the image of Jesus Christ is to be conformed in the image of God because Jesus is the express image of His Father. Furthermore, in **Hebrew 1:3 (KJV)** *Who being the brightness of his glory, and the express image of his person, and upholding all things by the word of his power, when he had by himself purged our sins, sat down on the right hand of the Majesty on high.*

God provided The Savior Jesus Christ to save us from death and connect us to Himself.

____

____

____

____

____

____

____

____

Jesus Christ, Our Savior

Mankind fell from the spiritual realm because of Adam's disobedience. Which led to mankind losing their position of righteousness, sonship as Sons of God, and living from the spiritual realm. Mankind needed a Savior; because of God's love, He provided His only begotten Son Jesus Christ to be the world's Savior. Jesus Christ is the only way to the Father.

In the Book of **John 14:6 (KJV),** *Jesus saith unto him, I am the way, the truth, and the life: no man cometh unto the Father but by me.* It's through Jesus Christ we can be connected   back to God and live from where we were meant to live from, which is the Spirit realm which is our divine position of righteousness as sons of God. The world needed a savior to redeem us back, and because of God's love towards us, He sent His Son to be the Savior of the world. And in **1 John 4:14 ((KJV),),**

And we have seen and do testify that the Father sent the Son to be the Saviour of the world.

The world was doomed to hell because we were separated from God, who is life.

The sinful nature we inherited from Adam has its wages, and it is death. That's why we needed a Savior, Jesus Christ, to give us God's gift, eternal life. Also, in **Romans 6:23 (KJV),** the scriptures state, "*For the wages of sin is death, but the gift of God is eternal life through Jesus Christ our God.*

Without God, we were dead in trespasses and sins. In the Epistle of **Ephesians chapter 2 (KJV),** Apostle Paul writes, "*You hath he quickened, who were dead in trespasses and sins.[2] Wherein in time past ye walked according to the course of this world, according to the prince of the* *power of the air, the Spirit that now wor-keth in the children of disobedience: Among whom also we all had our conversation in times past in the lusts of our Flesh, fulfilling the desires of the Flesh and the mind, and were by nature the children of wrath, even as others.*

Without God, we were dead in trespasses and sins, walking according to the course of this world, according to the prince of the power of the air. We were living from the sinful nature, fulfilling its lust of the Flesh, and we were by nature the children of wrath. But because of God's great love towards mankind, He sent His Son Jesus Christ to save us so that we should no longer be children of wrath but brought us back to our sonship and position of righteousness and start living from the spiritual realm again in fellowship with the Father.

God didn't send Jesus to condemn us. Condemn means to sentence, find guilt, damn, doom, and declare unfit for use. God didn't send Jesus to condemn or declare us unfit or to make us feel guilty, but He sent Jesus to save us.

This is evidenced in the Gospel of **John 3:16-17 (KJV)** *For God so loved the world, that he gave his only begotten Son, that whosoever believe in him should not perish, but have everlasting life. For God did not send His Son into the world to condemn the world, but the world through Him might be saved.*

John 3:17 amp For God did not send the Son into the world to judge (to reject, to condemn, to pass sentence on) the world, but the world might find salvation and be made safe and sound through Him.

God loved the world and sent His only begotten Son to die for the whole world so the whole world might be saved.

The Greek word for saved is "sozo," which means; healed, prospered, and delivered. God sent His Son to heal, prosper and deliver the world but not to condemn it. Jesus didn't come to judge us to be wrong, to pronounce us guilty, to sentence us, or to pronounce us unfit but to save us, which is to heal. Prosper and deliver us. So, if you are saved, God has already healed, prospered, and delivered you. God didn't send His Son to judge or condemn us but to save us (heal, deliver, and prosper us) because He loved us.

In the Book of Romans 5:8 (KJV), *God commendeth his love toward us, in that, while we were sinners, Christ died for us.* God demonstrates His love towards us in that while we were still sinners, Christ died for us. God demonstrated His love towards us by sending His Son, Jesus Christ, to die for us while we were still sinners. His love was demonstrated towards us from 2000 years ago. We need to believe in Him and receive everything He did for us through Christ Jesus by Faith. God has already saved the world, and by believing that God raised Jesus from the dead and confessing with the mouth of the Lord Jesus, the world will be saved and be reconciled back to God.

Furthermore, in the Book of **Romans 10:9 (KJV),** Apostle Paul continues and says, *That if thou shalt confess with thy mouth the Lord Jesus, and shalt believe in thine heart that God hath raised him from the dead, thou shalt be saved.*

Jesus brought God's peace and goodwill toward men.

In the Gospel according to **St. Luke, 2:14(KJV)** *Glory to God in the highest and on earth peace, goodwill towards men.*

The scripture didn't say "peace towards man to man, but God towards man because we were separated from Him, so through

Jesus, we have peace with God. God reconciled the world to favor with Himself through His Son, Jesus Christ.

In **2 Corinthians 5:19 (KJV),** To wit, that God was in Christ, reconciling the world unto himself, not imputing their trespasses unto them; and hath committed unto us the word of reconciliation. It was God (personally present) in Christ, reconciling and restoring the world to favor with Himself, not counting and holding (men) their trespasses (but canceling them) …What situation were we in when God was reconciling the world to Himself? We were dead in our trespasses and sins, walking according to the course of this world, conducting ourselves in the lust of the Flesh. We were naturally children of wrath, but God's love was greater to reconcile us to Him and make us alive through His Son, Jesus Christ. So, God has already reconciled everybody to

Himself through Jesus Christ, who was the propitiation for the sins of the whole world.

According to 1 John 2:2 (KJV), *He is the propitiation for our sins: and not for ours only, but also for the sins of the whole world.* God loves the whole world, and He is not willing that any should perish but ALL should come to repentance.

And in 2 Peter 3:9 (KJV), *He the Lord is not slack concerning his promise, as some men count slackness; but is longsuffering to us-ward, not willing that any should perish, but that all should come to repentance.*

He sent Jesus to be the atoning sacrifice for the sins of the whole world; all the sins of the world are forgiven; everybody's past, present, and future sins are forgiven, But the world must believe and receive what Jesus did for us by Faith by first confessing with their mouth the

Lord Jesus and believe that God raised Jesus from the dead. They will be saved and be rescued from death to eternal life.

And in the Book of **Romans 6:23 (KJV),** *For the wages of sin is death, but the gift of God is eternal life through Christ Jesus.* The word "sin" in this verse doesn't mean the action of sins but sin nature, as we spoke earlier in Romans 5:12,19. The sinful nature or old man's penalty is deaths. First death is the separation from God, physical death and eternal .

But God loved us so much to send His Son to die for us so we can be reconciled to Him and have eternal life. The world has already been reconciled to God through our Savior Jesus Christ, now all we have to do is to believe and receive our Savior by Faith by confessing Him as Lord and believing that God raised Him from the dead and we are saved: healed, delivered, and prospered.

By being reconciled to God, we receive His life and start living from our spiritual realm with Him as our Father because we are born of Him.

How We Started in The Spirit

We have seen that all human beings were born from spiritual death because we were born from the lineage of Adam, who was separate from God, according to Romans 5:12,19. So, to be reconciled to God, we needed a Savior, Jesus Christ, who is the only way to the Father. The Bible says the only way to God is through Jesus. In The Gospel according to Saint **John 14:6 (KJV),** *Jesus said to him, I am the way, the truth, and the life. No one comes to the Father except through Me.*

The only way to the Father is to be born again by confessing and believing that God raised Him from the dead. Jesus told Nicodemus unless a man is born again, he cannot see the kingdom of God. In Additionally, **John 3:1-8 (KJV),***There was a man of the Pharisees named Nicodemus, a ruler of the Jews:[2] The same came to Jesus by night, and said unto him, Rabbi,* *we know that thou art a teacher come from God: for no man can do these miracles that thou doest, except God be with him.[3] Jesus answered and said unto him, Verily, verily, I say unto thee, except a man be born again, he cannot see the kingdom of God.[4] Nicodemus saith unto him, how can a man be born when he is old? can he enter the second time into his mother's womb, and be born?[5] Jesus answered, Verily, verily, I say unto thee, except a man be born of water and of the Spirit, he cannot enter into the kingdom of God.[6] That which is born of the Flesh is Flesh, and that which is born of the Spirit is Spirit.[7] Marvel not that I said unto thee, Ye must be born again.[8] The wind bloweth where it listeth, and thou hearest the sound thereof, but canst not tell whence it cometh, and whither it goeth: so is every one that is born of the Spirit.*

1. Physical birth is of the Flesh, where we are born from our earthly parents.
2. Spiritual birth is being born from the Spirit.

To be born from the Spirit, we need to be Born from God, who is Spirit According to John 4:24 God is a Spirit and they that worship him must worship Him in Spirit and truth.

We needed to be born of the Spirit to be connected to our Heavenly Father. Jesus came to restore us to the Father so we can live from the spiritual realm with The Father just like Adam did before the fall. He was living from the spiritual realm with God, His Father.

In John 1:1 The word is God, and the word is Spirit according to **John 6:63**

(KJV), *It is the Spirit that quickeneth; the Flesh profiteth nothing: the words that I speak unto you, they are Spirit, and they are life.* Spiritual birth is being born from the Word of God, the Spirit.

1 Peter 1:23 (KJV), says, *you have been regenerated (born again), not from a mortal origin (seed, Sperm) but from one is immortal by the ever living and lasting Word of God.*

Furthermore, Romans 10:9 (KJV), states, That if thou shalt confess with thy mouth the Lord Jesus, and shalt believe in thine heart that God hath raised him from the dead, thou shalt be saved. So, when we accept Jesus Christ as Lord by confessing with our mouth the Lord Jesus and believe in our hearts that God raised Jesus from the dead, we are spiritually born again. Which is being *saved.*

The moment you are spiritually born again, you become a new creature in

Christ (2 Corinthians 5:17). That Spirit is joined to the Lord. In **1 Corinthians 6:17 (KJV),** *But he who is joined to the Lord is one Spirit with Him.* And in **2 Corinthians 5:17 (KJV),** *Therefore, if any man be in Christ, he is a new creature: old things are passed away; behold all things are become new.*

Your life from that moment you got saved, begun from the Spirit, and that's who we were. In Christ Jesus, we should live from who we are in the Spirit cause we are not in the Flesh but in the Spirit (Romans 8:9). We are Spirit with a soul living in a body. **1 Thessalonians 5:23 (KJV),** *And the very God of peace sanctify you wholly, and I pray God your whole Spirit and soul and body be preserved blameless unto the coming of our Lord Jesus Christ.*

This scripture shows us that we are triune beings, we are a Spirit with a soul, and we live a body. Our body is not the real us. When a person dies on earth the body goes back into the soil/dust, but the Spirit continues to live.

A body without the Spirit is dead (James 2:26). We are in the Spirit which is the Spirit of Christ. Accordingly, **Romans 8:9 (KJV),** *But ye are not in the Flesh, but in the Spirit, if so be that the Spirit of God dwell in you. Now if any man has not the Spirit of Christ, he is none of his.*

The Spirit of Christ is the spirit of His son According to **Galatians 6:5 (KJV),** *To redeem them that were under the law, that we might receive the adoption of sons. And because ye are sons, God hath sent forth the Spirit of his Son into your hearts, crying, Abba, Father.*

So, God is your Heavenly Father. We are born from God, so we are Sons of God in Christ. The new creature in

Christ, the Spirit, is the real us. See yourself as a Son of God in Christ. You are a Spirit being in the Spirit as a Son of God which is our identity.

We are back to God's purpose. Living from the spiritual realm with our Heavenly Father . That's how we began in the Spirit, and Our lives are now in the spiritual realm in Christ. We are now Sons of God, and we should see ourselves as Sons of God, and God is our Father. We live from the Spirit as sons of God who are in glory. Jesus brought us back to glory according to **Hebrews 2:11,** and we possess the glory. Therefore, to add clarity, in the book of **2 Thessalonians 2:14 (KJV),** *Apostle Paul says, whereunto he called you by our gospel, to the obtaining of the glory of our Lord Jesus Christ.*

The word obtain is "peri poiesis" in Greek which means possession, one's property..

.We are sons of God back to the spiritual realm with our Father in glory.

____

____

____

____

____

____

____

____

____

____

____

____

____

____

We Continue How We Started

Our spiritual lives as Sons started in Faith. By Faith, we were saved. In **Ephesians 2:8 (KJV),** *For by grace, you are saved through Faith; and that not of yourselves: it is the gift of God.*

The word Greek word for saved is "sozo." which means;

1. Healing
2. Deliverance and
3. Prosperity

We are blessed with all spiritual in Christ. So, when we became sons of God, our sins were forgiven (Ephesians 1:7, Colossians 1:14), and we were healed, delivered, and prospered. We received everything through Jesus Christ when we started our new life in the Spirit as Sons of God. Accordingly, **Ephesians 1:3 (KJV),** *Blessed be the God and Father of our Lord Jesus Christ, who has blessed us* *with all spiritual blessing in the heavenly places in Christ.*

Salvation also took place when we were born again, sons of God. Salvation is soteria" in Greek which is

1. healing
2. deliverance
3. safety
4. soundness
5. preserved
6. prosperity
7. wholeness

So, by Faith, we are healed, delivered safe, preserved, and prospered; we have a sound mind and wholeness.

Through Jesus, we have everything, and again just the way we started in Faith is the way to receive everything we need by Faith. In the book of **Romans 5:2 (KJV),** *By whom also we have access by Faith into this grace wherein we stand and rejoice in the hope of the glory of God.*

Faith accesses everything we need. We have also received the Faith of the Son of God. In **Galatians 2:20 (KJV),** *I am crucified with Christ: nevertheless, I live; yet not I, but Christ liveth in me: and the life which I now live in the Flesh I live by the Faith of the Son of God, who loved me and gave himself for me.*

We started in the Spirit by Faith, believing God's word, and continue living by Faith because we were made righteous the moment we got saved. In **2 Corinthians 5:21 (KJV),** *For he hath made him be sin for us, who knew no sin; that we might be made the righteousness of God in him.*

Righteousness, in a broad sense, is the state of him who is as he ought to be, righteousness, the condition acceptable to God. The doctrine concerning how man may attain a state approved by God. Integrity, virtue, purity of life, rightness, the correctness of thinking, feeling, and acting. We were made righteous, which is the same name as the just. The Bible says the Just shall live by Faith. And in **Romans 1:17 (KJV),** *For therein is the righteousness of God revealed from Faith to Faith: as it is written, the just shall live by Faith.* **Galatians 3:11 (KJV),** *But that the law justifies no man in the sight of God, it is evident: for the just shall live by Faith.* In the Book of **Habakkuk 2:4 (KJV),** *Behold, his soul lifted is not upright in him: but the just shall live by his Faith.*

God has already given us everything we will ever need; all we need to do is believe and receive. We are already saved through Faith, so now we should continue our lives in Faith. Believing in what God has done for us through Faith. Our lives are a life of Faith. The Epistle to the church at Corinth, **2 Corinthians 5:7 (KJV),** Apostle Paul writes, *For we know that if our earthly house of this tabernacle* *were dissolved, we have a building of God, an house not made with hands, eternal in the heavens.[2] For in this we groan, earnestly desiring to be clothed upon with our house which is from heaven:[3] If so be that being clothed, we shall not be found naked. [4] For we in this tabernacle do groan, being burdened: not for that we would be unclothed, but clothed upon, that mortality might be swallowed up of life. [5] He that hath wrought us for the selfsame thing is God, who also gave us the earnest of the Spirit.[6] Therefore, we are always confident, knowing that, while we are at home in the body, we are absent from the Lord:[7] (For we walk by Faith, not by sight:)*

That's why it's important to know the moment we got saved, we started our lives in the spiritual realm in Christ. We no longer live from the Flesh but from the Spirit Romans 8:9. Walking in agreement with our Heavenly Father. And in **Romans 8:8 (KJV),** *So, then they that are in the Flesh cannot please God.*

Change happened in the spiritual realm. The Greek word for "please" in strongs definition is "Aresko," which is to be agreeable. As sons of God, we always agree with our Father in Heaven. The moment we got saved we started our lives from the Spirit. Many people continue to live the same way they used to live because they never knew their lives had begun in the Spirit.

Believers need to know we are in the Spirit, living from the spiritual realm with our heavenly Father. We are alive unto God, so we walk from who we are in Him. That's why we walk by Faith and not by sight.

Through Adam, we were dead, separated from God. We walked according to the course of this world according to the prince of the power of the air, the Spirit that now works in the children of disobedience (Ephesians 2:2). In Christ, we are made alive unto our Father living in unbroken fellowship with Him. So, in the book of **Romans 6:11 (KJV),** *Likewise reckon ye also yourselves to be dead indeed unto sin, but alive unto God through Jesus Christ our Lord.*

Even so, consider yourselves dead to sin *and* your relation to it broken but alive to God. [living in unbroken fellowship with Him] in Christ Jesus. Start Seeing Yourself from Who You Are in The Spirit.

You Are Accepted

You Are a Son of God

You Are Righteous

You Are a Spiritual Being Living in The Spiritual Realm.

Heavenly Father Is Your Father

____

____

____

____